...IF YOU TRAVELED WEST IN A
Covered Wagon

by Ellen Levine

illustrated by Elroy Freem

SCHOLASTIC INC.

New York   Toronto   London   Auckland   Sydney

For Uncle Allie and Anne

Special thanks to Elaine Johnson, historian of Soda Springs,
Idaho, for her advice and assistance and to Telza Gardner of the
New York Public Library.

ISBN 0-590-45158-8

12 11 10 9 8 7 6 5 4 3 2 1   2 3 4 5 6 7/9

Printed in the U.S.A.   09

First Scholastic printing, August 1992

CONTENTS

Introduction

One hundred and fifty years ago there was no railroad that went all across the country. There were no cars or buses or airplanes. The only way to travel across the country was to ride a horse, or if you went with your family, to travel in a covered wagon.

In the 1840s and 1850s, thousands of people traveled West. So if you lived at that time, there was a chance you might have traveled in a covered wagon.

This book is about traveling and living in a covered wagon. It tells what it was like to be one of the early pioneers to travel to Oregon.

What was the Oregon Territory?

In the 1840s the Oregon Territory was made up of the land that is now the states of Oregon, Washington, Idaho, and parts of Montana and Wyoming.

Back then nobody knew if the Oregon Territory was going to be part of America or if it was going to be part of England. Both countries had built forts in the territory. At the forts, trappers and Indians sold animal furs and skins, such as beaver, marten, and muskrat, and bought tools and supplies.

America and England agreed that Oregon would belong to the country that could get more of its people living in the new land. So to make Oregon part of America, many Americans had to go there to live. Oregon finally became a state in 1859.

Why did some people want to travel all the way to Oregon?

Back in the 1840s you heard about faraway places by reading newspapers or hearing stories told by visitors who came from the distant places. This is how people learned of a land on the other side — the west side — of the Rocky Mountains. That land was called Oregon.

Stories told about Oregon made it sound like a magical place. Flowers bloomed all year. The land was good for farming. And there was plenty of land that you could get for free. There were tall trees and big forests, and rivers and streams filled with fish.

So the very name *Oregon* made people think of starting new adventures.

What was a covered wagon?

A covered wagon was a wagon with a white rounded top made of cloth. The cloth was called canvas and was rubbed with oil to make it waterproof. It was stretched over big wooden hoops that were bent from one side of the wagon to the other.

There were drawstrings in the front and back of the canvas. If you pulled the strings tight, you could close the ends up to keep out the rain or wind. The canvas could also be rolled up on the long sides, so that you could get a breeze on a hot day.

The bottom part of the covered wagon looked like an ordinary wagon with one difference: The front wheels were smaller than the back wheels. That made it easier to make sharp turns.

Inside the wagon there were hooks on the wooden hoops. On them you could hang milk cans, guns, bonnets, spoons, dolls, jackets, and anything else there was room for.

Underneath the wagon between the back wheels there was a hook with a bucket full of grease hanging down from it. The grease was rubbed on the wheels so that they would turn smoothly.

In the front of the wagon there was a wooden board to sit on.

The covered wagon was pulled by oxen or mules or horses. Many pioneers used oxen because they were stronger than mules and horses.

Covered wagons were also called prairie schooners. Can you guess why?

A schooner is a boat that sails on the seas. The big white canvas cover on the wagon looked like a huge sail. And if the grass was tall enough to hide the wheels, the wagon looked like a big boat sailing across the grassy green waves.

What was a wagon train?

A wagon train was a group of covered wagons that went together on the long trip West. The wagons would travel in a single line so that from a distance they looked like a slow-moving train. If the trail was wide enough, they would sometimes spread out to get away from each other's dust.

At night the wagons would form a big circle with the front of one wagon facing the back of another. Children would often play inside the wagon circle after dinner and just before bedtime.

Did anybody lead the wagon train?

Yes. When pioneers gathered their wagons together at the start of the trip, they elected a leader. This leader, or captain, would blow the horn or whistle to wake everybody up in the morning. He was also the one who decided when you would stop for lunch and at the end of the day.

The captain, with a few others, would often ride a little in front of the wagon train to see what was ahead on the trail. Then they would ride up and down the wagon line to make sure that everything was okay.

Usually there was a council of about six to ten people who would meet at night with the captain to talk about how the trip was going. Each person would report on different problems:

- A wagon wheel had broken and the family needed someone to help make a new one.

- Somebody's flour barrel had gotten all wet and muddy crossing the river, and the family needed to get some flour from anyone who could spare a little.

- A group of men had to be organized for the next day's buffalo hunt.

The captain and the council would plan who would stand guard at night to protect the animals and warn the people if anything was wrong.

What was a "trail guide"?

Some wagon trains hired trail guides. These were people who had made the trip before and knew the way. Usually they had been fur trappers and traders out West for many years. When they came back to the East, they had special knowledge that was very helpful to the pioneers.

The guides would know the best places to cross the rivers. They knew how far you had traveled and how much more you had to go. And they taught the pioneers some of the tricks of the trail, which you can read about in this book on page 73.

Some of the guides even wrote books about how to travel West. This meant that the captain and the council of a wagon train could study a guidebook and learn about the best way to go.

One of the most famous guides was a man named Dr. Marcus Whitman. He was a doctor and a missionary. He and his wife, Narcissa, built a home in the Oregon territory. If you look at the map on page 7, you will see where they lived.

Dr. Whitman was a trail guide for the first big wagon train to go to Oregon in 1843. It was made up of about 120 wagons. Because he had made the trip before, he was very helpful to the pioneers who were going for the first time.

Dr. Whitman believed that the wagons could go over the mountains in Oregon. No covered wagons had ever gone across those mountains before. But the pioneers trusted Dr. Whitman, and they made it!

What kinds of people traveled West?

Many different kinds of people went to live in the new place called Oregon.

Farmers wanted to go to find good new land. Storekeepers wanted to go to set up new shops. There were carpenters and bakers and blacksmiths. There were missionaries and shoemakers and artists and lawyers. There were doctors and teachers and almost anyone else you can think of who might want to try something new.

You were especially lucky if people who knew many of these different things were in your wagon train. Then it was like carrying your whole town with you on the trip.

Sometimes people who didn't start out with you on the trip were there when you arrived at your new home. That's because babies were born on the trip!

If you had a new sister or brother on the trip, the wagon train would stop for a day or two. Usually several of the women knew how to help when babies were born. And there in the middle of a new country would be a new person.

The travelers, including the new babies, were called pioneers because they were the first group of people to move into a new land and make a new home.

What would your family bring in their covered wagon?

As much as you could pack in. It was necessary to leave behind everything that you didn't really need, especially if it was heavy.

The oxen and horses pulling the wagons had a hard time just walking across the country. If the wagons were too heavy, the oxen could die from exhaustion.

It was very important to try to figure out how much food you would need for the five or six months you would be traveling. There was no supermarket you could go to when you ran out of supplies. So you would bring flour and yeast for baking bread. Your family would also bring crackers, cornmeal, bacon, eggs, dried meat and dried fruit, potatoes, rice, beans, and a big barrel of water. They might even have some chocolate for special treats.

If your family had cows, you would bring them along for milk and meat.

Your family also knew they would be able to hunt for more meat on the trail, and that they would find wild berries and honey and some vegetables along the way.

Pioneers made their own clothing, so your family brought along cloth to sew with, needles, thread, pins, and scissors, and leather to fix worn-out shoes. You had to make your own repairs, so you brought saws, hammers, axes, nails, string, and knives.

For daily chores you would bring things like soap, wax for making candles, lanterns, and washbowls.

Many people brought tents to sleep in outside the wagons. If they hunted buffalo on the trail, they would often use the skins for making blankets. With the fur on the inside, a buffalo skin was warm and soft.

It was also important not to forget medicines, in case somebody got sick on the trip.

Nobody forgot plates, knives, forks, spoons, cups, and pots and pans. They were kept in a special box attached to the back of the wagon.

What was the best time of year to start the trip?

This was a very important question. The answer had to be just right or there might be many problems on the trip.

The answer is that you had to start from Independence, Missouri (or nearby), in May because of the oxen and cows and the weather. Can you guess why?

If you started *too early* the spring rains would have made so much mud that the wagon wheels would get stuck. Then you might have to spend days digging yourself out.

Also, if you started too early, the grass would not have grown tall enough and thick enough to feed all the cattle along the way. After the pioneers ran out of the hay they had brought with them in their wagons, the cattle would grow weak and might even die from hunger.

The whole trip took about five or six months. So if you started *too late* you might be caught crossing mountains in a heavy winter snowfall. This happened to some wagons. On one trip some of the pioneers had to camp in the mountains through the winter until spring, when the snows melted. Then they were able to travel on. Some died from cold and hunger during the long wait.

The perfect time of year to start was in the spring after the rains, when the sun was shining and the grass was growing tall.

How would you cross rivers when there were no bridges?

It wasn't easy crossing rivers back in the 1840s. The covered wagons started West from towns on the Missouri River. So, often the very first thing you had to do on the trip was to cross a river. One place to start from was a town called Independence.

Independence was a small town with a few farms, some stores that made and fixed wagons and wheels, and many people sleeping in tents waiting to begin their trip West.

Large flat boats called scows would take the wagons across the Missouri River. But the horses, cows, and oxen had to swim across because they couldn't fit on the scows. The covered wagon had blocks of wood placed in front and in back of its wheels so that it wouldn't roll off the scow.

Once the wagons crossed the Missouri River into Kansas and Nebraska, the pioneers were in Indian territory. Sometimes Indians had rafts and would ferry you across rivers. You would have to pay them with money or beads or something else they wanted.

Sometimes you crossed rivers on rafts that you would help to build. You would tie together willow branches and put thick, long grasses called rushes on top. Then you would roll the wagon onto the raft and ferry it across the river.

Most of the time you would seal the wagon tight by filling in all the cracks in the wood with tar or candle wax mixed with ashes. Children helped make the wax paste and put it in the open spaces in the wooden planks. Sometimes you would cover the inside with animal skins to make the wagon even more waterproof.

Then you would take the wheels off and push the wagon into the water. It would float across the river like a fat, flat boat.

Children usually rode inside the wagon. Two or three men also rode inside and steered the wagon with long poles. Others would ride horses into the water and try to steer the wagon from the outside. It could take over an hour to get across a river this way. If there were a lot of wagons in your wagon train, it sometimes took five days for everybody to get across.

Sometimes wagons tipped over and everything inside was lost in the river. And sometimes the river flowed so fast that a wagon was dragged away and you couldn't catch it. If that happened, you and your family would probably ride with other families in the wagon train.

How far would you travel in a day?

On many days you would travel ten to fifteen miles. If it was muddy and raining hard, you might make one mile in a whole day.

Today if you are driving in a car on the highway, you usually travel fifty-five miles in one hour. In a covered wagon it might take you five or six or even *seven* days to go as far as you can go today in one hour!

You would usually have to get up very early to start traveling in the wagons. Most people got up around four o'clock in the morning, when it was still dark.

First they would start the fire so that they could cook breakfast. Then they would round up the cattle and start to load up the wagons with the tents, blankets, pots, and pans.

The wagons would start moving by seven o'clock in the morning and travel until lunchtime. Then you would rest for an hour or two. After lunch you would travel again until about four or five or sometimes six o'clock at night. Finally you would stop until the next day.

After five or six months, you would have traveled more than two thousand miles. Today that would take about three or four days in a car, and three to four hours in an airplane!

Would you ride in the wagon for the whole trip?

No. In fact you probably wouldn't ride for even most of the way. If you ever had a chance to ride in a covered wagon for more than an hour, you would know why.

Too bumpy! There were no smooth highways or roads back in the 1840s. Sometimes you made your own trail by being the first wagon to go over a piece of ground. Other times you rode in the ruts made by other wagon wheels.

You could feel every bump when you sat in the wagon. There were no cushioned seats — just wooden boards covered with a few blankets.

Much of the time you would walk next to the wagon. The wagons traveled very slowly, so you could easily keep up with them. When your feet got very tired, then you might climb up and ride for a while. And sometimes you might want to ride in the wagon just to get the view from high up.

The drivers would often walk alongside the oxen. They didn't use reins. They would shout and sometimes use a whip. But you wouldn't hit the animals. You would just crack the whip over their heads to make them go the way you wanted.

What were the dangers and difficulties of the trip?

One of the biggest problems was mud. Sometimes it would rain for days on the prairies and then there would be mud, mud, and more mud.

You could sink right up to your knees in mud. And if *you* could sink, so could the oxen, cows, and horses.

When the sun came out, most of the mud would dry up in a few hours. Sometimes, though, the wagon wheels would still be stuck.

Then the children would help gather long grasses. You would lay them across the ground in front of the wagon wheels. Then the oxen would pull from the front and people would push from behind. The wheels would turn onto the grass and slowly come up out of the mud.

The opposite problem is when the ground is too dry. Then there would be dust — so much dust that it would get in your eyes, your mother's eyes, your father's eyes, and the cattle's eyes. The dust would be so thick that you could hardly see your hand in front of your face.

When that happened, sometimes you had to stop traveling because you couldn't see the trail at all. Most of the time, though, you just kept going anyway and hoped you were going the right way.

Another problem was sickness. Some people became very ill with high fevers and aches and pains. Both grown-ups and children got diseases called cholera and malaria. Sometimes they died on the trip. You would pass many grave markers by the side of the trail as your wagon went by.

Today there is medicine to keep you from getting these diseases, and to cure you if you do get them. People didn't know as much about diseases and medicines in the 1840s as they do today.

Where would you sleep?

Sometimes you would sleep in the wagon, sometimes under it, sometimes in a tent, and sometimes out in the open under the stars.

There wasn't enough room in the wagon to bring a mattress for everyone in the family. So if there was one mattress, usually your mother and father would sleep on it. They might leave the mattress in the wagon if there was enough room, or they might put it in a tent and sleep there.

Babies and little children usually slept in the wagon.

If it was raining, it wasn't easy to keep completely dry. The best place was inside the wagon. The next best place was in the tent. You would probably get a little wet if you put your blankets under the wagon and went to sleep there.

If it looked like it might rain when your parents set up the tent, they would dig a ditch around the tent so that water would run off into the ditch and not under the tent.

If you were going to sleep under the wagon when it was raining, your mother and father would wrap your blankets in an oilskin, which is a piece of cloth that has been rubbed with oil and is waterproof.

In good weather the nicest place to sleep was out in the open under the starry skies. If you lay on your back and looked up at the faraway stars, you could pick one, call it *Oregon*, and try to think how long it would take you to get there. Oregon would seem almost as far as that star.

What kinds of clothes did people wear?

Everyone wore simple clothes. You would get too dirty and dusty traveling all day to wear fancy clothes. Clothes had to be made of strong material because they had to last for many months. There were no stores along the way where you could buy new clothes.

Very often women would carry along rolls of cloth in their wagons. Then they could make new shirts or dresses when the old ones were torn or too worn to wear anymore.

Boys wore shirts and pants made of cotton or buckskin, which is leather made from the skin of a deer. It is soft and strong, and yellow or gray in color.

Girls wore skirts or dresses, usually made of brightly colored cotton called calico or gingham. It had stripes or checks or flowers in different colors.

You spent so much of the time walking alongside the wagons that it was very important for everyone to wear sturdy, strong shoes. But the trip was so long that they often wore out. Then you would hope that someone in the wagon train was a shoemaker. If not, your mother and father would help fix the worn-out shoes.

Another important thing to have was a hat or bonnet. Remember that in those days there were no sunglasses, and the sun was very bright and hot. So boys would wear hats with wide brims, and girls would wear bonnets that helped protect their eyes.

What would you eat?

For the first part of the trip you would eat mostly what you brought in the wagon — biscuits, potatoes, bacon, dried meat, crackers, dried fruit, cornmeal, beans, and eggs.

Then, just when there were no hard biscuits left, you would start eating "fried bread." There were no real ovens to bake bread in. So your mother would mix dough and then fry it in a pan.

At first it was nice to have something new. But then it got very boring to eat the same thing over and over again. You would be glad to travel into new territory where there were wild onions and berries of all kinds, and where you might catch catfish in the rivers and trout in the mountain streams.

If you were carrying eggs in a bumpy wagon traveling across rivers and up and down hills and over mountains, how would you keep them from breaking?

Some of the pioneers put the eggs in the flour barrel, making sure the eggs didn't touch each other. The only problem with this was that your hands would get all white whenever you reached in to dig out an egg!

Everybody wanted butter because it made the dry biscuits and fried bread taste better. The pioneers would get milk for making butter from the cows they brought. But after traveling all day, making dinner, rounding up the cattle, fixing broken things, and doing all the other chores, there wasn't much time left to make butter.

But the women discovered an easy way to make it. They would hang a milk can from the wagon hoops or tie it to the side of the wagon. As the wagon bumped along the trail, the milk bounced around so much that in a few hours when you opened the can there was a ball of butter at least an inch thick, and lots of smaller pieces. The butter had made itself!

After traveling for many weeks, the wagon trains moved into buffalo country. And that meant new and delicious food.

How did you make the buffalo meat last a long time?

The buffalo is a very big animal with lots of meat on it. There was too much meat to eat all at once. And so the pioneers learned from the Indians how to dry the meat and keep it for a long time. The way to dry it was called "jerking."

First the meat was cut into strips about one inch thick. Then the strips were heated over a very low fire for several hours. Another way to dry the meat was to put it out in the sun. It would take about two days to dry.

Usually the pioneers could not stop and wait two days while the meat dried. So they would tie strings on the outside of the wagon from the front to the back and hang the strips of meat over the strings. It looked like fringes hanging down. The meat would dry while you kept on traveling West.

How would you build a fire if you didn't have any wood?

Out on the plains you would sometimes travel for days without seeing any trees or wood that you could use to build a fire.

And so the pioneers had to find something else that would burn easily. They discovered that dried buffalo droppings — called buffalo chips — made a hot, clean fire with little smoke and no smell.

Usually the children would take baskets and collect the buffalo chips before dinner. It could take three full baskets to cook a meal.

It often got very windy on the plains. So the safest way to make the fire was to dig a trench ten inches deep, six inches wide, and about two feet long. Then you would put the chips down in the trench and light them with matches or by setting off gunpowder.

When the wagon trains reached the Rocky Mountains, there were no more buffalo chips. And it was still sometimes hard to find wood. So the pioneers burned dead sagebrush branches and even the sage roots.

Children would gather the dead sage the night before so that you could have a fire for cooking breakfast.

What happened if you met Indians on the trail?

For most of the trip West, people traveled through land that Indians lived in. There were many different tribes, such as the Blackfoot, Cheyenne, Pawnee, Crow, Sioux, Bannock, and Shoshone.

Some of the Indians were friendly and some were not. All of them were surprised to see the big wagon trains moving slowly across their lands.

If you met friendly Indians, you could trade with them. You would give them things they wanted, and they would give you things you wanted.

One thing all the pioneers wanted was moccasins. These were soft but strong shoes made of deer or buffalo skin. They were often decorated with colored beads.

The Indians wanted cloth, red paint, glass beads, and metal fishing hooks.

If the Indians were not friendly they might try to steal the cattle and horses. That's why it was very important to have the guards stay awake at night and watch over the wagon train.

Sometimes a guard would accidentally fall asleep or be caught by the Indians and tied up. Then the Indians would take the cattle and horses. Often the pioneers could pay the Indians for the cattle to get them back. This was called paying a ransom.

Sometimes a group of Indians got very angry that all these strange people were crossing their lands. So they would fight with the pioneers. When that happened, all the wagons would form a circle. Younger children would usually lie down inside the wagons so that they wouldn't be hurt during the fighting. Then everybody who knew how to use a gun would help out.

Most of the time in the 1840s, though, there was not much fighting. The real wars with the Indians began in the 1850s and 1860s. That's when the pioneers began to build their homes all across the lands where the Indians lived.

Would you go to school during the trip?

It all depended on how many children there were in the wagon train. If there were many, in some wagon trains they would get together when the wagons stopped for lunch or dinner and an older person would go over lessons with the children.

On some wagon trains, children would study their readers and learn arithmetic from their parents or older brothers and sisters.

Many families were able to bring a few books with them in their wagons, so that you could practice your reading.

Some people said that the whole trip was one great big school because you were learning new things every day. You might learn the names of flowers or animals you had never seen before.

You would learn about fixing things when they broke down, because you couldn't just go to a store and buy something new.

You would learn about cooking outdoors and tying up the animals so that they had enough room to move around and eat but couldn't run away.

There were so many new things to learn that by the end of the trip, you knew a lot more than when you had started out.

What chores would you have to do?

Everybody worked very hard during the long days of traveling West. Children had lots of things to do:

They milked the cows

and fetched water from the rivers

and watched the cattle when they walked behind the wagons

and helped cook the food

and washed dishes

and helped skin and prepare the buffalo or deer or wild turkey when they were caught and collected wood or buffalo chips in baskets to help make the fire

and shook out the blankets and quilts in the fresh air

and hung the beef jerky to dry.

Some of it was hard work, some easy. But most of the chores were interesting because instead of living in a house, you were living in a covered wagon and things had to be done in new and different ways.

Could you have fun on the trip?

If you like going places that you have never been before — and if you like seeing things for the first time that you have only heard or read about — you would have had a lot of fun. For there was something new to see and hear almost every day.

During the day there would be a chance to explore a little if you didn't go too far from the wagons.

Then at night, after you helped with dinner and cleaned up the dishes, many interesting things happened.

Usually there was someone in the wagon train who knew how to play a harmonica or a fiddle. Everybody would gather around and sing songs and dance.

Sometimes you would sit by the camp fire and listen to stories — maybe even a ghost story!

And if the sun was shining in early July, the July 4th celebrations were something very special. Everybody prepared for days for an Independence Day party.

Most people didn't carry an American flag with them on the trip, and so they had to make one. You would need something red and something white and something blue. So you would look for just the right material.

First you would take a sheet for the white of the flag. In one wagon train they cut up a red shirt to make the stripes and a blue jacket for the stars to be sewn on. By the end of 1845, you would have needed twenty-eight stars.

If you knew how to sew, you could help to make the flag. And before you knew it, "Old Glory" would be ready!

Then came the big feast. Buffalo and antelope meat, sage hens (a little bit like chicken), and jackrabbits. And, of course, potatoes and beans and rice and a special treat of pickles if someone had brought them on the trip. For dessert there were different kinds of cakes and chocolate.

Everybody ate so much they thought they would never eat again. It was a day you would remember for a long, long time.

Would you see any wild animals?

Absolutely. The biggest animal that you would see would be a buffalo. If a herd came near the wagon train, you might see hundreds and hundreds at one time. They would run close together and kick up a lot of dust. You could feel the earth shaking as they went by.

One young woman named Helen Carpenter traveled West in a covered wagon and wrote down what she saw. She wrote that when an old buffalo was shot and fell on its side, it was so big that you couldn't see the head of a nine-year-old boy standing behind it!

You would also see prairie dogs. They were very interesting to watch because they lived in prairie-dog cities. At least that's what it looked like — lots of "doorway" holes in mounds all over the ground.

When you came near a prairie-dog city, you knew it right away. The prairie dogs would sit outside their doorways on their hind legs and watch you.

If you came too close, they would run inside. It seemed as if they were curious about who you were, but didn't really want to meet strangers.

Wherever there were prairie dogs, there were rattlesnakes and owls. They seemed to be next-door neighbors, but were not always friendly. Sometimes a rattlesnake or owl would catch a prairie dog and eat it.

You would also see or hear other wild animals. At night if you heard a chorus of howls, it could be wolves or coyotes. And in the daytime you might see jackrabbits, wild turkeys, sage hens, and lizards. You would probably see an antelope running, but if you didn't look quickly, it might be gone. That's because they are very fast runners.

If you think of mosquitoes as wild animals, then you would see and feel a lot of them.

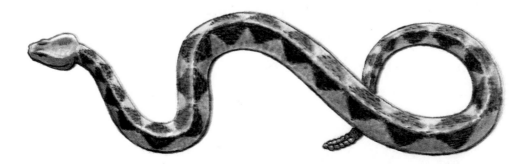

Could you send a letter or receive one?

Back in the 1840s there were no post offices west of the Mississippi River, so it wasn't easy to send or receive a letter. But there were a few ways that you could do it.

Sometimes people would send letters to you at a fort on the trail. Some supply wagons going West would carry the letter to the fort and leave it there for you to pick up.

At the forts you might be able to leave a letter, which another wagon train would carry back home for you. In some places you were charged money to send a letter, and in some places you were charged money to receive one.

Today, of course, only the sender of the letter pays money for the stamps.

There were no envelopes for letters in those days. You would fold the letter up and drip some melted wax on the edge. When the wax cooled and hardened, the letter could not be opened until you broke the wax. That way you would know that nobody had read your letter.

There was no television or radio back in the days of the covered wagons. People learned about what was going on in the world from reading newspapers, magazines, and letters.

Before there were big cities in the West, all the newspapers and magazines came from the East. They had to be mailed out West just like letters.

By the time you got all the way to Oregon, it might take two years for a letter to get to you. And it could take just as long for a newspaper to get all the way out West. You might not know who was president of the United States until two years after the election!

If you ran out of supplies, could you get more?

Sometimes. Along the trail there were a number of forts where the wagon trains would stop. You would usually stay over at a fort for a few days to rest up. It was also a chance to let the oxen, horses, and cows have a rest.

After you left Independence, Missouri, the first big fort you reached was Fort Laramie. It took about forty days to reach the fort. Most wagon trains got there at the end of June.

There were lots of things to do when you got to Fort Laramie. It was a time to fix the wagons, do the laundry, and buy or trade for new supplies.

Usually there were Indians at the fort. They set up their tents, which were called tepees (tipis), outside the walls of the fort, and traded with people at the fort.

The pioneers wanted to buy sugar, flour, coffee, cloth, leather, and other things they had run out of.

Sometimes the fort had extra supplies. But sometimes a wagon train had arrived before you and bought out just about everything. You would be out of luck then.

It might take you almost thirty more days to get to the next fort, called Fort Bridger. This fort was named after a man called Jim Bridger, who was an early fur trader and trapper. He even helped guide some wagon trains west.

Another fort before you reached Oregon was Fort Hall. From there you traveled west and north to Oregon. Some pioneers left the Oregon Trail at Fort Hall and went south and west to California instead. On either trip you would still have to travel at least two more months!

Was it hard driving the wagons over mountains?

Yes! Some of the mountains were very high. You might have to borrow your neighbor's oxen to help pull your wagon up a high mountain. It would take a long time to get up the mountain this way. When you got to the top, the oxen had to be untied and sent down to help the next wagon.

You also had to be very careful going down steep mountains. The pioneers put poles through the wheels to keep them from turning and rolling too fast. They would also tie one end of a rope to the back of the wagon and tie the other end around a tree or big rock at the top of the mountain. If you loosened the rope at the top very slowly, you could keep the wagon from racing down the hill.

The heavier the wagons, the harder it was to cross the mountains. So often you would see chairs or tables or boxes that people had left behind on the trail to lighten their loads.

Sometimes the pioneers even had to cut their wagons down so that they were left with a cart that had only two wheels. It was easier to take a two-wheeled cart over some mountains than a whole wagon.

You just hoped that wouldn't happen to your wagon.

Without road signs, how would you know where you were?

It wasn't always easy. It may be hard to imagine that you could get lost, but out on the open prairie everything looked the same — huge fields of waving grass. One pioneer wrote that everybody was "so turned around that they were uncertain which was the right way to go."

Sometimes you got help from trees, or rocks, or water holes. In places on the trail there were big rocks with funny shapes, or water that looked and tasted unusual, or trees that were bent in strange ways.

The early fur trappers and traders who had gone West had given names to many of these things. So when the pioneers traveled in their covered wagons, they looked for these landmarks. When you saw one, you knew you were going in the right direction. You also knew how far you had come.

One famous landmark was called Chimney Rock. It was a tall column sitting on a bed of rock and rose about 500 feet from the ground into the air — about forty stories high. You can probably guess why it was called that name. When you reached Chimney Rock, you had traveled some 550 miles from Independence, Missouri.

Another famous landmark was Independence Rock. Some people say that it got that name because early travelers reached it on July 4th and celebrated Independence Day there.

It was a great rock shaped like a turtle's back, and you could see it from far away. Independence Rock was a favorite place to climb. You also knew who had traveled before you, because many people carved or painted their names into the rock. In one spot a whole wagon train joined together and painted "THE OREGON COMPANY — 1843" on the rock.

Children loved one landmark called Soda Springs. It had bubbling water that you could drink. When you bent your head near the water, the bubbles tickled your nose.

And there was a place called Steamboat Springs. Here water came rushing up two to three feet in the air from cracks in the rock. It was blowing, splashing and spraying, whizzing and sizzling, and making the puff-puff sound of a steamboat.

There was also a very scary landmark that Jesse Applegate called Devil's Backbone. If you think about how narrow your backbone is, you will understand why this was a place you would never forget.

When Jesse's wagon train reached Devil's Backbone in 1843, the trail was very narrow. On the left side the cliff went down about a thousand feet. On the right side it was worse — the cliff went all the way down to the Snake River, which seemed about a mile down. (A mile is 5,280 feet!)

At some spots on Devil's Backbone there was room for not much more than the wagon. Then everybody got out and walked in front of and behind the wagons until the trail got wider.

If you travel West today, you can see all of these places yourself.

What is the Continental Divide?

If you drew an imaginary line along the top of the Rocky Mountains from the north to the south, you would have drawn the Continental Divide. This is the place in the United States where the great rivers flow in different directions. On the west side, all the rivers flow toward the Pacific Ocean. On the east side, they all flow toward the Atlantic.

The wagons crossed the Continental Divide at a place called South Pass. It was an opening in the mountains that was so wide, it didn't seem as if you had crossed anything very important. Then you reached a spot called Pacific Springs. There you could watch the first waters on your trip flowing west!

You knew you were at least halfway to Oregon.

What special tricks of the trail did the pioneers learn?

When you lived for five or six months in a covered wagon, traveling almost every day, you had to learn or invent new ways to do things.

Here's a problem the pioneers had to solve: What could you do when the oxen's feet got sore? If *you* got tired from walking and your feet were very sore, you could climb up into the wagon and ride for a while. But what were the oxen supposed to do?

The pioneers learned a "trick" from the Indians. First you cut a small piece of animal skin. Then you make small holes all around the edges and put a string or narrow strip of leather through the holes to make a drawstring.

You then put the side with the hair around the ox's foot and pull the string up tight and tie it like a shoelace. After two days of wearing these "moccasins," the ox's feet would be better.

It was also very important to know how to find your way back to the wagon train if you got lost out on the prairie. The trail was usually close to the river. So you would be safe if you could find your way to the water.

If you had gone out exploring on the prairie, it wasn't always easy to see the river. Although the land looked flat, the rivers usually ran in a valley. Sometimes the sides of the river banks were sixty feet high.

The secret was to follow the buffalo tracks. The buffalo walked in single file — many rows of them — to the river to drink. They used the same paths over and over again. So their paths were sometimes ten inches deep and a foot wide. You couldn't miss them.

The pioneers also learned how to leave messages on the trail for wagons coming after them. Sometimes notes were written on the bones of cattle that had died along the way.

Another way to leave messages was to cut a slit in a stick, put a piece of paper with your message on it into the slit, and stand the stick in the ground near the trail so that the next wagon train could see it.

Sometimes messages told you that a cow had been lost and would you please watch to see if you could find it. Other notes might tell you that there was a good place to camp up ahead. Sometimes notes just sent greetings to friends.

Do you remember the other tricks of the trail described in this book?

- How do you make butter while the wagon is moving?
- How do you keep eggs from breaking as you ride over bumpy trails?
- How do you dry meat to make it last a long time?
- How do you make a fire without wood?

How do we know what it was like to travel West in a covered wagon?

We know a lot about the wagon trains from diaries that the pioneers wrote. When you keep a diary, you try to write down what happens every day. You write about what you see and think. You can write down anything that interests you, including what other people say and do.

Many diaries were written by grown-ups, but sometimes children wrote them, too. Helen Scott was eleven years old when she traveled West in a covered wagon, and she kept a diary.

Jesse Applegate was also young when his family went to Oregon. He didn't write a diary then, but he wrote about the trip when he grew up. One thing he remembered was how big the prairie-dog cities were. He said he thought some seemed as great as New York City!

And Helen Carpenter was nineteen years old when she went West and wrote in her diary that buffalo meat was delicious.

You can learn a lot about the Oregon Trail from reading diaries, because each person wrote about different things. If you were a shoemaker, you might write about how the Indians made moccasins. If you were a doctor, you might name all the plants you saw that would make good medicines. If your wagon wheel broke, you might write about how to make a new one.

What do you think you would have written about?

Is there anything left of the old Oregon Trail?

Today you can drive on highways over much of the old Oregon Trail. Along the way you can see some of the places you have read about in this book.

In fact, at many places on the old Oregon Trail you can stand in the wagon ruts made by the covered wagons that went West so many years ago.